Meditations on Relationships

۶ ۶ ۶

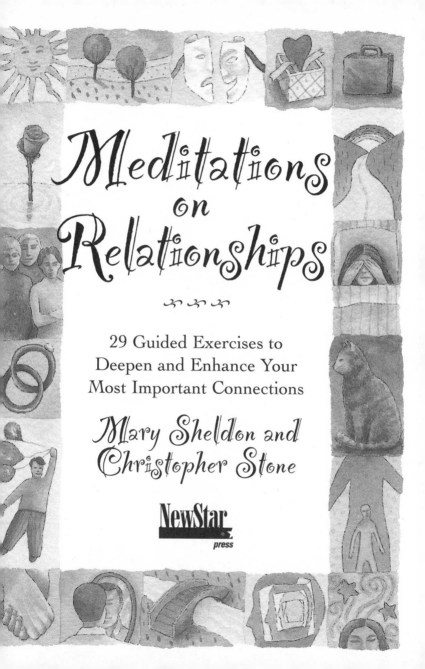

Meditations on Relationships

29 Guided Exercises to Deepen and Enhance Your Most Important Connections

Mary Sheldon and Christopher Stone

NewStar *press*

ISBN: 0-7871-1839-7

A NewStar Press Hardcover published by
NewStar Publishing a division of NewStar Media Inc.
8955 Beverly Boulevard, Los Angeles, CA 90048

Cover and text illustrations by Tanya Maiboroda
Text design and layout by Carolyn Wendt
Printed by Malloy Lithographing, Inc.

First NewStar Hardcover Printing: February 1999

10 9 8 7 6 5 4 3 2 1

Printed in the United States of America

For Rebecca Rowana
The angel in our midst

M.S.

For Mary Sheldon, Bob Van Dusen, Lizy Dastin,
and Rebecca Van Dusen
My Golden Family in the Golden Triangle

C.S.

Acknowledgments

Thank you, Beth Lieberman, and all the other people at NewStar Press, for your patient work on this "Meditation" series.

Thank you, my precious Bob, Lizy, and Rebecca, for your daily doses of comfort and joy. Never was wife or Mama so blessed.

Thank you, all those friends (especially Rose Casey) from whom I so greedily plundered ideas for areas of meditations. I hope you're happy with the results.

Thank you, dear Christopher, for triumphing once again.

And thank you, everyone who reads this book, for giving us your time. We give you our love.

Mary Sheldon

Believing myself to be lavishly blessed, a prayer of gratitude for life lives in my heart—where Carmen Montez, and my gratitude to her love-based teachings, also reside.

Quite simply, on a day-to-day basis, nobody gives me more energy, love, support, or time than David M. Stoebner.

Once again, I want to mention the cherished family to whom I've dedicated this work: Mary R. Sheldon Van Dusen, Bob Van Dusen, Lizy Dastin, and Rebecca Van Dusen.

My parents, Elsie and Phil Di Leo, who recently celebrated their sixtieth wedding anniversary, are among my greatest treasures. Ingrid Gundel Watson is not only a great friend, she is one of the most deeply good people I know. Loving, kind, considerate, and in all ways generous, Ingrid takes after her sainted father, Wilford E. "Wofford" Watson. On multiple levels, Dorris "Fifi" Halsey has been looking out for my well-being for many years. Jack Schober, Dick and Dee Lewis, Max Brown, Lisa and Tom Derthick, Dick, Holden, Lori Rasor, and Alexandra and Sidney Sheldon—much joy would be missing from life without you. And what would I do without Jose Garcia, Jr., Clara Abellard, Ashley, David, David IV, and Sharyn Crabtree, Paula Greenstein, Rusty MacLean, Lee Cowan and Marc Mantell, Ann, Angela, and Jaclyn Drown, Frank Schaffer, Stephen Jacobs, Charles Pierce, and Barbara and Chuck Crandall? My love to Rae Dawn Chong, Christopher Collet, Christopher Thomas Howell, John Mercedes III, and Charlene Tilton. Thinking about you brings back so many wonderful memories of days gone by. Welcome back, David Alexander Tolken. Mark Tanney, I miss you so much.

And thank you, Beth Lieberman, for making our business a pleasure.

Christopher Stone

Contents

MEDITATIONS ON FAMILY RELATIONSHIPS

MEDITATIONS ON WORK

SPECIALIZED RELATIONSHIPS

PERSONAL TABLE OF CONTENTS

Introduction

Welcome to *Meditations on Relationships*. We're so glad you're here.

I think we have a lot to offer you in this book—and it doesn't matter what your personal situation may be. You may be married or single, you may have a family of five or be childless; you may have parents living or parents gone to spirit, you may have coworkers or be unemployed; you may have brothers and sisters or be an only child. We're tried to put something for everyone in this book, and hopefully there will be a lot of inspiration for you.

Because relationships are so varied, not every reader is going to have the same meditation needs. Therefore, some do-it-yourself is going to come into play. We want you to design your own table of contents each month—one specifically tailored to you.

There are several meditations, (Meditations 1–7), which are about our relationship with ourselves and our relationship to God. Since these are relevant to everyone, we suggest that you do these every month, regardless of your personal situation—but after that you're on your own.

MONTH ONE

When you get this book, familiarize yourself with the table of contents and the meditations offered. Choose which ones seem relevant to you at the moment. Now turn to the section entitled Personal Table of Contents, "Month 1," and write your choices in the space provided, one meditation to be done per day. We have already filled in for you our seven suggested meditations, but you're even free to ignore these if you so desire. You're also free to adapt the meditations—if there's one in the romance section that you feel you could re-work and apply to a job situation, by all means do so. This is your book—use it as you like.

Then, day by day, do one of your chosen meditations until you've finished the course. (Obviously, the length of the course will depend on how many meditations you've chosen.)

SUBSEQUENT MONTHS

Whenever you're ready, repeat the process. You may have the same needs and may want to stick with the same meditations, or perhaps new situations may have opened up, requiring different ones. Just fill in a new table of contents, and you're off!

Have fun with this book. The meditations were prepared with much love, and I hope that all your relationships grow in joy.

Mary Sheldon
Los Angeles, California
July 1998

"There is one true happiness in life, to love and be loved."
—George Sand (1804–1876)

I tend to agree with Sand, née Dupin. I was raised to believe that health and good relationships in all areas of life are this world's greatest treasures. My parents, especially my father, attached little importance to fortune, power, fame, or social position. At the same time, he greatly prized health and close, loving relationships. How many times I heard him declare, "Money can't always buy happiness," or "If you don't have your health, you don't have anything," and "Without loving friends and family, life isn't worth much." So, I am most grateful to make a small contribution to the subject area of relationships.

Recently in several national periodicals, I have read that in polling people about relationships, the vast majority of those polled claimed that a healthy relationship with God was among their most important priorities. But many of those polled said they chose not to pursue things spiritual through organized religion. Instead, these people say they turn to metaphysical teachers, New Age instruction, and mental disciplines, including meditation, for their spiritual growth. The articles' authors found two primary reasons for their poll participants' lack of devotion to religion.

1. Many of those polled believe that religious teachers largely miss the point of religion and dishonor the Divinity by teaching a God who is calculating, judgmental, merciless, and vindictive. In other words, many religious teachers are preaching and teaching a God who is much easier to fear than to like, love, or respect.

2. Many Christians polled believed that so-called Christian denominations had long ago "missed the boat." The church was intended to be the medium of Jesus' message of hope, love, and tolerance, but instead, in an effort to consolidate and increase its power, the church has become the message, and the living Jesus has been lost along the way.

Regardless of the specific relationships you are pursuing, it is my prayer that love, and the peace that love brings, will be the cornerstones of your every relationship. Towards that end, this book can help.

Christopher Stone
Redondo Beach, California
July 1998

The Relaxation Technique

Before doing each of the exercises, we suggest that you begin with a relaxation technique. The One below is adapted from an exercise in Christopher's book *Re-Creating Your Self*. However, if you already have a technique you're comfortable with, by all means use that.

ॐ ॐ ॐ

Assume a comfortable position in a quiet, pleasant place; then close your eyes and begin.

Imagine that the muscles in your scalp and forehead are becoming very comfortable and relaxed. Your eyebrows relax, the area all around your eyes relaxes . . . the tiny muscles of your eyelids relax, and the relaxation continues to flow . . .

It spreads deep into the back of your throat, deep into your head and neck, deep into your shoulders . . .

Now your arms relax . . . first the upper arms, then the lower. You feel the relaxation spreading across the tops of your hands, sinking all the way through the palms, down the fingers . . .

Return your attention to your relaxed neck and shoulders. Let the relaxation flow into your chest and lungs. Your breathing becomes easy and gentle. Feel yourself becoming more deeply relaxed with each gentle breath. All outside sounds are unimportant.

Now let the relaxation spread deeply into your back. Feel it flow down to the small of your back, warming and loosening wherever it touches.

The relaxation spreads into your sides, your stomach. Feel the muscles of your stomach and hips relax.

And now your legs relax. The relaxation flows into your thighs and knees. Your calves relax, your ankles, your feet . . . the heels of your feet. And finally, even your toes relax.

Your entire body is at peace, and you remain perfectly aware and focused, ready for meditation.

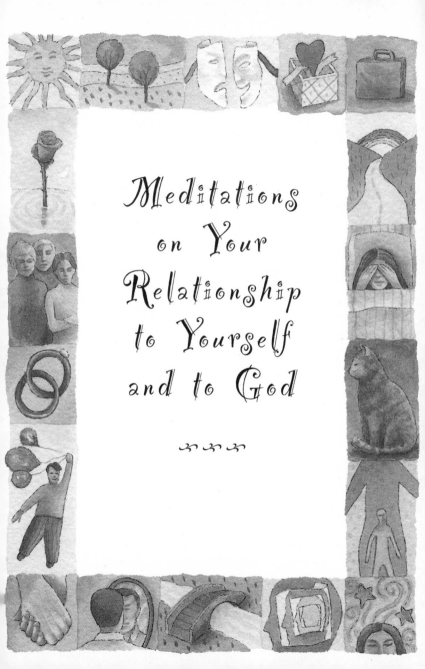

Meditations
on Your
Relationship
to Yourself
and to God

↭ ↭ ↭

MEDITATION 1

The Bottom Line

TIME REQUIRED: *five to ten minutes*

So many of our relationships—to our families, our friends, our daily lives, the world in general—seem, on the surface, to be outward-based. And yet there is one very special, very inward-based relationship that pretty much determines how all the others in your life are going to be. It is best summed up in the phrase, "As within, so it is without." Get this relationship on track, and you're virtually home free!

ॐ ॐ ॐ

1. Get comfortable, close your eyes, and do the relaxation exercise.

2. Do a quick run-through of the major areas of your life. Health, prosperity, relationships, your work situation, personal happiness, and any others that come to mind. For all those things that are going

well, congratulate yourself—remember that "As within, so it is without," and know that you are holding positive, healthy beliefs in these areas.

3. When you come to an area of your life that is causing you anxiety, stop. Take a few breaths. Again, remember that "As within, so it is without." Know that you are holding false and/or limiting beliefs in these areas of anxiety.

4. See the outward situation as if it were an image you are watching in a mirror. Since the scene is only something you are witnessing, and not actually experiencing, you are able to detach and evaluate it impersonally.

5. Ask your inner self why you have created this anxiety-producing situation. What "within" you is being manifested "without?" What false or unhealthy beliefs are getting in your way? What do you need to do to change the image?

6. Imagine the mirror image changing. Visualize the challenge being resolved, and the self you see in the mirror being confident and grateful.

7. Take a few deep breaths, open your eyes and end the exercise. Write down your realizations in the space provided.

MONTH 1

MONTH 2

MONTH 3

MONTH 4

MONTH 5

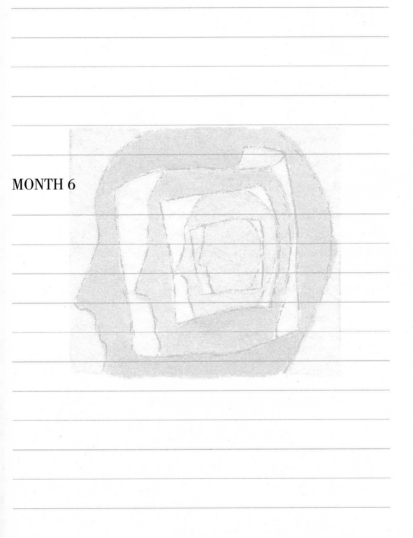

MONTH 6

MEDITATION 2

BIG I/little me

TIME REQUIRED: *five to ten minutes*

Often, our relationship to life is a fearful one. We can feel like tiny, insignificant creatures, powerless and victimized by the big, bad world and people around us. Here's a simple meditation to help you look beyond that self-image and allow yourself to remember that there is a giant within you.

ॐ ॐ ॐ

1. Get comfortable, close your eyes, and do the relaxation exercise.

2. Envision yourself as the character "me"—a person only three inches tall. Imagine how it would feel being so tiny. Let yourself feel powerless, terrified.

3. Using situations and challenges from your present life, have your "me" character ask questions about what's going on—always using him/herself as the

object. They might be questions like: "Why do things like this always happen to *me?* What does s/he think of *me?*"

4. Now stop being the victimized, terrified "me." Change into your "I" self. Feel yourself starting to grow. Grow and grow until you are enormous. Now look down at the once scary world and see that it is like an adorable dollhouse. Feel yourself calm and secure—know that no one can hurt you.

5. Have your "I" self ask the same questions that your "me" asked. Only now using yourself as the subject, not the object. You might ask "What do *I* need to learn from this condition?" "What do *I* think of this person/situation?"

6. Acknowledge that you have both the little me and the BIG I within you and that it is your choice as to which you will be.

7. Take a few deep breaths and end the exercise. Write your impressions in the space provided.

MONTH 1

MONTH 2

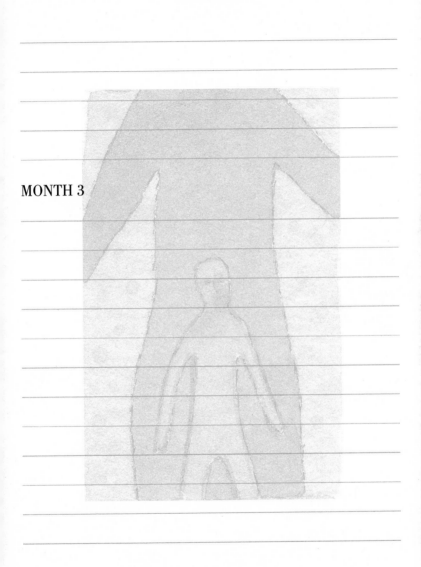

MONTH 3

MONTH 4

MONTH 5

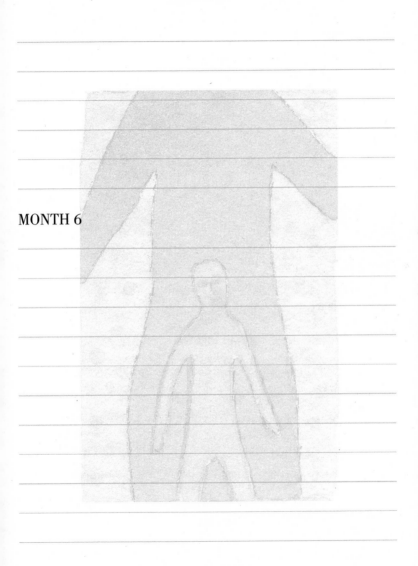

MONTH 6

MEDITATION 3

Oh, God!

TIME REQUIRED: *five to ten minutes*

Because God is Really All There Is, you can legitimately visualize God to be any vision of Good that you choose. You can create and cultivate a close, healthy relationship with a highly personal God, regardless of religious affiliation.

ॐ ॐ ॐ

1. Get comfortable, close your eyes, and do the relaxation exercise.

2. Envision God however you choose. Have fun with this one. Is God a glowing light, pulsing with warmth and love? Does God wear the face of an adored being you knew in this life? Is God music?

3. Thank your own personal vision of God for your life and for all of its blessings.

4. Silently tell your divine vision that your greatest desire is to grow into a closer relationship with It— and to better know the highest good for your life and for those lives that touch yours.

5. Take a few deep breaths, open your eyes, and end the exercise. Write down your divine vision in the space provided.

MONTH 1

MONTH 2

MONTH 3

MONTH 4

MONTH 5

MONTH 6

MEDITATION 4

Ask Nature

TIME REQUIRED: *half an hour*

Not every reader will have a romantic relationship, a spouse, siblings, children, or living parents. But, from cradle to grave, everyone will have a relationship with Nature—the dramatic, beautiful physical world which includes all living things. This simple meditation lets you experience Nature as the great, wise, permissive teacher it is meant to be.

Note: Save this exercise for a day when it is practical to be outside; then go to the most inspiring outdoor environment near you. If you live in a beach town, do this exercise on the beach. If you live in the mountains, go into the forest. If you are a city person, find a park or even just an outdoor bench on a reasonably quiet block.

ॐ ॐ ॐ

1. Get comfortable, close your eyes, and do the relaxation exercise.

2. Meditate for a moment on the nature of Nature. Realize that it is a friend to man, not a threat. Man is his own threat. Realize that Nature will not condemn you, nor will it criticize or judge you.

3. Think of the most important question you currently have about your life. Now, with gratitude and humility, ask Nature for an answer to that question.

4. Wait in patience for Nature to respond. Your answer may come on the breeze. It may penetrate your consciousness in a ray of sunlight, or it may come to you in a raindrop, or a foggy mist. Your answer may be delivered by the buzz of a bee, by the pleasant drone of a hummingbird, or even by the roar of a wave crashing upon the beach. You will get an answer. It may not be what you want to hear, but it will be somehow pertinent.

5. When the answer comes, end your meditation. Open your eyes, reorient yourself to your natural surroundings, then write the information you received in the space provided.

MONTH 1

Ask Nature

MONTH 2

MONTH 3

MONTH 4

MONTH 5

MONTH 6

MEDITATION 5

I Had a Dream

TIME REQUIRED: *fifteen minutes*

One excellent way to build a better relationship with yourself is to create specific dreams that will help you attain greater self-awareness and understanding. This meditation will help you do just that.

Note: This meditation is to be done just before you go to bed in the evening. You will need a pen/pencil and this journal at your bedside.

༄ ༄ ༄

1. Get comfortable, close your eyes, and do the relaxation exercise. Because this is a bedtime exercise, take care that deep relaxation does not segue into sleep.

2. Silently request a dream that will give you new self-awareness into some area of your life that needs improvement. Don't be afraid to be specific. If, for example, you tend to sabotage relationships, request

data on precisely why this is occurring. If you have problems creating prosperity, ask for information that will help you improve the situation.

3. Affirm, either silently or aloud, "Tonight I will have and remember a dream that will help me improve my life and build a better relationship with myself."

4. While still in your meditative state, mentally construct the dream you want to have. That is to say, envision yourself in the sleep-state, receiving the information you seek. Does a wise being tell you what you need to know? Do you hear it whispered in your ear? Do you read it in a book? Envision your sleep-self grateful for the information and eager to put it to good use.

5. End the meditation and go to sleep.

6. Immediately upon awakening, whether right after having the requested dream or in the morning, write down as many of the details of your dream as you can remember in the space provided. If you haven't had the requested dream, repeat your request until you get it or until the sought-after information comes to you in another way. If the information comes to you "out of the blue," it could mean that you had the specific dream you requested but that you did not consciously remember it.

MONTH 1

MONTH 2

MONTH 3

MONTH 4

MONTH 5

MONTH 6

MEDITATION 6

Be Your Own Better Half

TIME REQUIRED: *fifteen minutes*

Most of us have ideas about what being in a wonderful committed relationship will give us—things like companionship, comfort, security and love. People not in a relationship can spend years feeling that, until the perfect romance comes along, something is missing from their lives. For those of you in that situation, here is a great exercise. Its aim is to help you start being that "special person" in your life and start supplying more of your own needs. And for those of you who are already in a committed relationship, this exercise is for you, too—the more of your needs you can fulfill yourself, the less strain your relationship will have to bear and the more you can enjoy your partner for being simply who he or she is, not for what he or she can give you.

ॐ ॐ ॐ

1. Get comfortable, close your eyes, and do the relaxation exercise.

2. Mentally identify the qualities and traits of your "perfect partner." Is s/he always nurturing and supportive? Does s/he delight in treating you to special cultural and entertainment events? Does s/he surprise you with gifts? Does s/he consistently focus on your good traits, while refusing to dwell on perceived shortcomings?

3. Now plan to start being that "perfect partner" for yourself, not only on a special one day only basis but regularly. Think of ten things your perfect partner would do for you—and do them for yourself. Buy yourself flowers or that new designer cologne. Look in the mirror and tell yourself how special you are. Get yourself tickets to that hit musical you want to see. Give yourself hugs whenever you need them. Make yourself feel loved and special in as many ways as possible.

4. Take a few deep breaths, open your eyes, and end the exercise. Write down your wonderful plans for being your own better half in the space provided. Have fun!

MONTH 1

MONTH 2

MONTH 3

MONTH 4

MONTH 5

MONTH 6

MEDITATION 7

Reflect on This

TIME REQUIRED: *ten minutes*

There is a wonderful expression, "We see others not as they are, but as *we* are." And so often what we most dislike seeing in others is what we most dislike seeing in ourselves. Here's a meditation to help you come to terms not only with problematic relationships—but with yourself.

✂ ✂ ✂

1. Close your eyes, take a few deep breaths, and do the relaxation exercise.

2. Think of someone with whom you are having problems at the moment. Hold his/her image before your eyes. (For ease in reading, we will call the person "he.")

3. Ask yourself: What particular quality about this person is driving me crazy? His possessiveness? His jealousy? His laziness? His inability to love?

4. When you have your answer, let yourself become aware that the only reason you are able to recognize this quality in the other person is because it also exists somewhere in you. Think of a few instances in your life when you have also exhibited this quality.

5. Envision this quality as a child. Give it a face, a body. See it as a small part of you, only wanting to be accepted and loved.

6. Accept and love this part of yourself. Say silently, "I am a diamond with many facets. This quality is one of them. I accept it in myself, and I accept it in other people."

7. See yourself and the person with whom you are having problems, sitting on a seesaw. At first, see the seesaw bouncing helplessly up and down. Now slow it down in your mind until you and the other person are perfectly balanced together.

8. Take a few deep breaths, open your eyes, and end the exercise. Write down your impressions in the space provided.

MONTH 1

MONTH 2

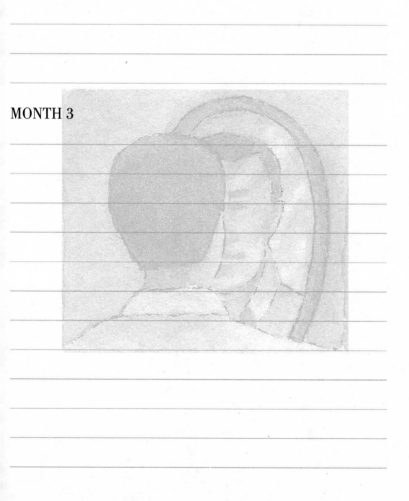

MONTH 3

MONTH 4

MONTH 5

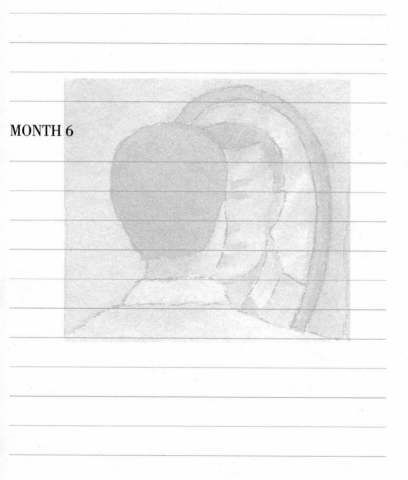

MONTH 6

Meditations
on Romantic
Relationships

❦ ❦ ❦

MEDITATION 8

Gifts of Love

TIME REQUIRED: *ten minutes*

There is a lovely song in the Steven Schwarz musical, *The Baker's Wife*, which speaks of the little "gifts of love" we can present to our partners. With those small gestures of affection, the whole is definitely greater than the sum of its parts, and you can leave a loved one feeling very cherished indeed.

❧ ❧ ❧

1. Get comfortable, close your eyes, and do the relaxation exercise.

2. Plan to make tomorrow a "gifts of love" day. (If tomorrow doesn't work for you, choose another day.) Come up with these little "gifts of love" you could bestow to make your partner's tomorrow that much better. Does he get up early to brew his own coffee? You get up even earlier to brew it for him.

Does she love to relax in a bath at night? As she is getting out, present her with a bath towel that you have just put in the dryer, leaving it warm and extra fluffy. Is beef stroganoff his favorite dish? Prepare it for him. Has she been talking about a book she wants to read? Stop by the bookstore after work and buy it for her. Give a massage. Write a love poem. Put the kids to bed. Do the dishes. Shine his/her shoes.

3. Open your eyes and end the exercise. Write down your gifts of love in the space provided.

MONTH 1

MONTH 2

MONTH 3

_____

_____

_____

_____

_____

_____

_____

_____

_____

_____

MONTH 4

_____

_____

_____

MONTH 5

MONTH 6

MEDITATION 9

Putting the Past to Bed

TIME REQUIRED: *ten minutes*

It is so important, when one romantic relationship is ended, to have closure on it—a sense of completeness, a feeling that you have learned from the experience and are now ready to progress. If that sense of closure isn't accomplished, if the necessary learning hasn't occurred, you might well find you are unconsciously making the same relationship mistakes ten, even twenty years down the line! Here's an exercise to help put the past to bed.

❧ ❧ ❧

1. Take a few deep breaths, close your eyes, and do the relaxation exercise.

2. Think about the first serious romantic relationship you ever had. Reflect on how it ended. Who ended it? What were the reasons? What were the issues that caused problems between the two of you? Think of

your life now. Are any of those issues still in evidence—either in your current romantic relationship or in your relationship with the world in general?

3. Repeat those questions with every subsequent serious relationship.

4. Notice if there are any patterns forming. Was jealousy always a key part of your breakups? Was it a lack of ability or lack of desire to commit? Did your partners tend to dominate in the relationship? Meditate on any patterns that emerge. Know that awareness can change things and that just because some trend has happened in the past doesn't mean it must happen again.

5. Once again, picture the first person you had a serious relationship with, and take in a deep breath. See yourself breathing in forgiveness—for yourself, for the other person, for the relationship as a whole

6. Hold your breath for a moment, then let it out. As you let it out, release the relationship. Say silently, "I am free of this relationship forever."

7. Repeat this with all your other relationships.

8. Take a few deep breaths, and open your eyes. Write down your experiences in the space provided.

MONTH 1

MONTH 2

MONTH 3

MONTH 4

MONTH 5

MONTH 6

MEDITATION 10

Taken for Granted

TIME REQUIRED: *ten minutes*

One of the saddest things that can happen in a marriage, or in any committed relationship, is, unhappily, one of the things that happens most. We start to take our partner for granted. Not only does this make him or her feel unappreciated, but it also robs us of many opportunities for enjoying the relationship.

৵ ৵ ৵

1. Get comfortable, take a few deep breaths, and do the relaxation exercise.

2. Call your partner to mind. See him or her standing in front of you, smiling. Now remember some of the things that first attracted you. Was it her sensitivity? His washboard abs? Her generosity? His always keeping his word? Chances are, those qualities are still there, and chances also are, you've been taking them for granted.

3. Think of other qualities and traits that you love about your partner. Do you love the way he listens to the story of your day before going on about his own? Do you love the way she's always patient with the kids? Do you like the way he always offers to drive?

4. Mentally thank your partner for being so wonderful, and promise not to take these marvelous qualities and traits for granted.

5. Take a few deep breaths, and end the meditation. Write down some of your partner's wonderful qualities and habits in the space provided, but don't stop there. Why not compose a long list on attractive stationary, filled with twenty or so things that you most love about your partner, and then present them to him or her. Every few months update the list, and renew your vow not to take your partner for granted!

MONTH 1

MONTH 2

MONTH 3

MONTH 4

MONTH 5

MONTH 6

MEDITATION

11

The Onion

TIME REQUIRED: *ten to fifteen minutes*

Like an onion, feelings come in layers and can sometimes cause a lot of tears. If you're feeling angry at someone you love, here's an exercise that can help you peel off the anger and get down to the more positive feelings underneath.

৯৯ ৯৯ ৯৯

1. Get comfortable, close your eyes, and do the relaxation exercise.

2. Get in touch with the anger you are feeling. Pretend that the person with whom you are angry is standing in front of you. Let him or her know, in a few well-chosen sentences, exactly why you are so upset.

3. Now look more deeply into your feelings. Almost always, anger is a mask for fear. Ask yourself what you are afraid of in this relationship. (The thing

that is causing you anger will help you identify the fear.) Is it fear of being abandoned? Fear of being trapped? Fear of losing your own identity? Do your best to identify the fear, and once again, mentally tell your loved one about your feelings.

4.   Now peel off one more layer. Underneath the fear, there is yet another set of feelings—love and understanding, both for yourself and for the other person. Use what you have learned about your fears to help you get to the place of love. See both you and the other person as vulnerable beings, doing your best. Acknowledge the love, let the warm emotions come flooding, and once again, tell the other person about your feelings.

5.   Take a few deep breaths, and end the exercise. Write about your experiences in the space provided.

MONTH 1

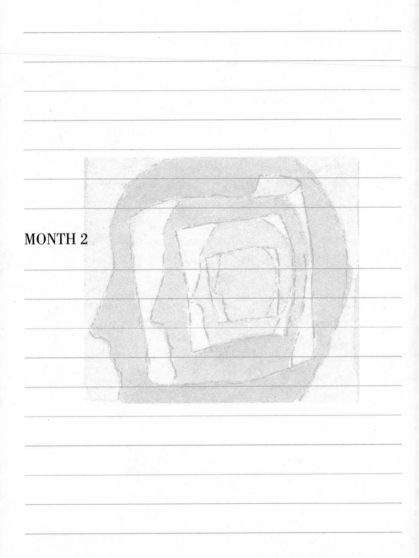

MONTH 2

MONTH 3

MONTH 4

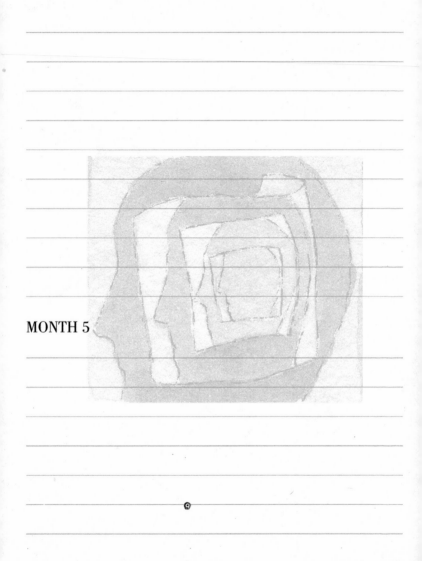

MONTH 5

MONTH 6

MEDITATION 12

Win-Win

TIME REQUIRED: *ten minutes*

So often, even the best-intentioned relationships can be beset by power struggles—about big issues and small—and these are struggles that neither side can win. Worse, they can sour a relationship more quickly than anything else. Remember, it takes two to tango (and tangle). Here is an exercise to help you let go your end of the power-struggle dance.

જી જી જી

1. Close your eyes, get comfortable, and do the relaxation exercise.

2. Think of something that your partner really wants but, for whatever reason, you are not allowing him or her to have. Does your husband want his night out with the boys? Does your wife want you to come home earlier from work so you can spend time

together? Does your husband want his mother to move in with you two? Has your girlfriend been begging you to quit being a musician and get a job on Wall Street?

3. Meditate on your partner's desire and your reasons for not wanting to grant the request. Does it threaten you in some way? Does it mean a lot of extra work for you? Does it represent an unwanted change in your routine? Accept these reasons. Love and understand yourself for feeling the way you do.

4. Now meditate on your partner's reasons for wanting the request. Try to see beyond the request itself to the need underneath. Is he or she really asking for love? Feeling frightened? Feeling unfulfilled and on a short leash? Love and understand your partner for feeling the way s/he does.

5. Change your focus. Stop looking at the situation from the human point of view and look at it from the spiritual. Realize that we are all on Earth to grow. Ask yourself what this issue is trying to teach you. In what ways could its resolution help you and your partner grow? See it as an opportunity for being more flexible and loving. Decide to make it into a win-win situation for you and your partner.

6. Think of one or more creative ways to handle the conflict in such a manner that both you and your

partner end up with something you need. In some cases, (letting your husband have the night out with the boys for example) you might find that it would help your spiritual growth simply to say yes to the request. So say it gracefully, and make the experience pleasant for yourself by doing something special when your partner is out. You might visit one of your friends, perhaps someone your partner does not really enjoy being around.

With other issues, you might find that, while you don't feel comfortable saying yes to the request itself, (your partner's wanting you to quit music and become a stockbroker?) you can still address her underlying need, in this case, the need for more financial security. Perhaps you two can start a business together—or think of ways to make your music more lucrative.

Note: The point is not to "give in" or to be a martyr in any way. It's to be a little more flexible for your partner's sake, for your own, and for the sake of your relationship.

7   Take a few deep breaths, open your eyes, and end the exercises. Write down your flexible win-win possibilities, and, if appropriate, share them with your partner.

MONTH 1

_____

_____

_____

_____

_____

_____

_____

_____

_____

_____

_____

_____

_____

_____

MONTH 2

_____

_____

_____

MONTH 3

MONTH 4

MONTH 5

MONTH 6

MEDITATION 13

Leaving Lonesome Town

TIME REQUIRED: *ten to fifteen minutes*

Many Baby Boomers remember the hit song, "Lonesome Town," by Ricky Nelson. Are you currently visiting that town "where the broken hearts stay?" Use this meditation to ankle out of Lonesome Town and discover there's a complete life waiting for you—even if the person you love leaves.

࿐ ࿐ ࿐

1. Get comfortable, close your eyes, and do the relaxation exercise.

2. Think about this: Most often, loneliness and depression follow a romantic breakup because we see the person who has left as the source of our goodness and completeness. Is this true for you? If so, identify the ways.

3. Replace that insecurity with the following affirmation: "All the goodness I can ever have originates

with me, within my consciousness, and not with any-body else."

4. Think about this: It is society which indoctrinates us into believing we're not complete unless we are tied to someone else. Have you bought into this belief? If so, identify the ways.

5. Replace this viewpoint with the following affirma-tion: "Whether single or partnered, I am created complete. Nobody can either add to me or take any-thing away. I am, as I have always been, and always will be, perfect, unified, and entire."

6. Take a few minutes to connect with your sense of personal completeness, and bless the person who has left you.

7. End the exercise, and write your impressions in the space provided.

MONTH 1

MONTH 2

MONTH 3

MONTH 4

MONTH 5

MONTH 6

MEDITATION 14

How Deep Is Your Love?

TIME REQUIRED: *ten to fifteen minutes*

Few would disagree that a loving partner, either within a traditional marriage or within a less traditional union, is among this world's greatest blessings. And if we are wise, we will actively and constantly seek new aspects of our partner's selfhood to cherish and love.

৯৯ ৯৯ ৯৯

1. Get comfortable, close your eyes, and do the relaxation exercise.

2. Bring your partner's image before your eyes. Now focus on one facet of his or her personality that has caused your feelings of love to deepen over time. Perhaps it's something small—like her/his consistently prompt payment of bills. Or maybe it's something larger, like his or her not being prone to alcohol abuse, anger, violence, or infidelity. Give thanks for

this trait, and plan on telling your partner how much you appreciate it.

3. Next, turn your attention to yourself. Think about a wonderful but too infrequently expressed quality or talent of your own—a facet of yourself that could cause your partner's affection for you to deepen. Are you a whiz at planning the perfect vacation? Are you a secret songwriter? Can you, if you set your mind to it, remain beautifully calm in stressful situations? Don't keep these qualities from your loved one any longer! Think of ways you can express them.

4. Bless your primary relationship. Mentally thank your partner for all that s/he adds to your life. Envision you and your partner continuing to grow in love together.

5. End the meditation and open your eyes. In the space provided, write down the love-deepening quality you have identified in your partner and also the quality in yourself that you have decided to express more often.

Note: Each month, come up with new qualities!

MONTH 1

MONTH 2

MONTH 3

MONTH 4

MONTH 5

MONTH 6

MEDITATION 15

Chakra Blending

TIME REQUIRED: *half an hour*

You will need a partner for this meditation. For those of you who already do chakra work, this exercise may take it to a new level. For those who don't, this will get you started. This is a wonderful exercise for increasing intimacy—physical, emotional, and spiritual—between you and a lover.

Chakras, according to yoga philosophy, are the body's seven power points, and each point is associated with a specific color and quality.

ॐ ॐ ॐ

1. Get with a partner, either undressed, or loosely dressed. Lie down together facing each other on a bed or the floor.

2. Be very still for a few minutes. Breathe in unison. Feel your partner's breathing.

3. Lightly touch each other on the small of the back. (The first chakra.) Visualize your energies merging. See streams of clear red light coming from each of you and blending. Feel yourself being linked to your partner through your double connection to the Earth.

4. Lightly touch each other around the genital area. (The second chakra.) Again, visualize your energies merging. Picture streams of clear orange light coming from each of you and blending. Feel yourself being linked to your partner as your sexuality and creativity grows.

5. Lightly touch each other in the solar plexus. (The third chakra.) Visualize your energies merging. See streams of clear yellow light coming from each of you and blending. Feel yourself being linked to your partner as the needs of your ego and personality are soothed and softened by the other, yet letting your individuality remain pure.

6. Lightly touch each other in the heart area. (The fourth chakra.) Visualize your energies merging. See streams of clear green light coming from each of you and blending. Feel yourself being linked to your partner through love—love for the world, and especially love for each other.

7. Lightly touch each other in the throat area. (The fifth chakra.) Visualize your energies merging. See streams of clear pale blue light coming from each of you and blending. Feel yourself being linked to your partner through perfect, unclouded communication. Know that all issues between you are speedily and harmoniously resolved.

8. Lightly touch each other in the area of the third eye. (The sixth chakra.) Visualize your energies merging. See streams of dark blue light coming from each of you and blending. Feel yourself being linked to your partner through your spirituality. Know that having this partner in your life is speeding up your growth and that you have chosen each other for the highest intentions in the world.

9. Lightly touch each other on the top of the head. (The seventh chakra.) Visualize your energies merging. See streams of clear light coming from each of you and blending, not only with each other, but with God. Feel yourself and your partner being united, together, to All that Is.

10. Let your hands drop to your sides. Continue breathing in unison. After a few minutes, end the exercise. Write down your impressions in the space provided.

MONTH 1

MONTH 2

MONTH 3

MONTH 4

MONTH 5

MONTH 6

Meditations on Family Relationships

༄ ༄ ༄

MEDITATION 16

Freeing Your Child

TIME REQUIRED: *ten to fifteen minutes*

Raising a child is surely one of the most challenging jobs on earth, and one of the most difficult issues lies in the area of parental expectations. We all want the best for our children, but what's "best" is a personal call. Parents often have an ideal (secret or otherwise) of exactly how their children should behave, how they should spend their time, where they should go to college, what they should do when they grow up. When these expectations are not fulfilled, so much unnecessary damage is created—for the child, for the parent, and for the relationship. Here is an exercise to help parents ease up a little.

꿍 꿍 꿍

1. Take a deep breath, close your eyes, and do the relaxation exercise.

2. See your child as he or she is now. (For ease in reading the exercise, we'll call the child "he.") See him

104

smiling at you (punk haircut and all!) wanting your friendship and approval.

3. Now visualize a cloud of smoke beginning to thicken around him. This "smoke" is made up of your expectations. See it start to choke your child.

4. Say silently, "I release you. I release you from my expectations. I release you to yourself and to your highest good. Be as you need to be not what I want you to be." Watch the cloud of smoke disappear. See your child running to you and hugging you gratefully.

5. Tell this child five things that you love about him. Mention to him things about him that are even better than you expected.

6. Talk with him about one particular expectation that he isn't meeting, the one about which you feel the most disappointed. Is it his choice of friends? His poor grades in school? His being ungrateful for all you've done for him? Hear what he has to say on the subject. Then tell him how you feel. Finally, take a deep breath, and let that expectation go.

7. Now go forward, and visualize your child as an adult. See him happy and successful on his own terms. Feel very proud of yourself for being such a wonderful and supportive parent.

8. Take a few deep breaths, and end the exercise. Write down your impressions in the space provided.

MONTH 1

_____

_____

_____

_____

_____

_____

_____

_____

_____

_____

_____

_____

_____

MONTH 2

MONTH 3

MONTH 4

MONTH 5

MONTH 6

MEDITATION 17

The Family Plan

TIME REQUIRED: *ten to fifteen minutes*

It is standard procedure in business to set up a plan for the future, envisioning where you would like your company to be in five years and then breaking the goals down into bite-size steps that can be accomplished. How rarely people extend this careful planning to their family life. Far too often family life is lived on a daily, catch-as-catch-can basis, with no goals set. Here is an exercise to help you set up a family business plan.

ॐ ॐ ॐ

1.   Get comfortable, close your eyes, and do the relaxation exercise.

2.   Reflect on your family life as it is now. Think about such issues as: How much time do you spend together? Do you have any shared interests? Is your house a peaceful place to live in, or is there a lot of

fighting? Does each member of the family have a say in what happens?

3. Bless your family, as it is now. Think of one area in which you believe family life could be improved.

4. Mentally put yourself five years into the future. Envision your family life as completely fulfilling and happy with the issues that needed to be improved now resolved.

5. Make a simple five-year plan to get to this goal. (Example: Let's say your issue is that you feel your family doesn't spend enough time together. Here's what your five-year plan might be: Year One: start eating one meal a day together. Year Two: arrange your schedule so that you do one special activity with each family member once a week. Year Three: arrange a "family time" once a week, in which you all do a shared activity—going to a restaurant, seeing a movie, etc. Year Four: find a hobby you can all enjoy together. Year Five: save up time and money for the most exciting family vacation you can manage.)

6. Take a few deep breaths, open your eyes, and end the exercise. Write down your big five-year goal and the year-by-year strategies on how to get it in the space provided. (Each subsequent time you do the exercise you can either refine your goals or pick a new area that you'd like to improve.)

MONTH 1

MONTH 2

MONTH 3

MONTH 4

MONTH 5

MONTH 6

MEDITATION 18

He Ain't Heavy, He's My Brother

TIME REQUIRED: *fifteen to twenty minutes*

For good or ill, our relationships with our siblings are some of the most important in our lives. Many metaphysicians believe that, before coming into this life, while we were still non-physical, we chose not only our parents but also our brothers and sisters. Whether or not you believe this, this meditation may give you insights into this close and complex relationship.

కు కు కు

1. Close your eyes, breathe deeply, and do the relaxation exercise.

2. Summon up an image of a sibling. (*Note:* If you have more than one, start with the oldest and work your way down every subsequent time you do the meditation. Also, for simplicity's sake, we will refer to the sibling as "he.")

3. Mentally travel upwards, through a golden tunnel, to pure spirit—to shortly before you were born into this lifetime. You and your parents-to-be are planning your future life together, and you have all just chosen to have this sibling enter the group. What are the reasons for your choice? What will this being offer you? What will you offer him? What lessons will he and you together teach your parents?

4. Now travel back into your childhood. What were your relations like with your sibling? Did you get along? If not, do these same conflicts still trouble you two now? Do they extend into your relationships with other people?

5. Think back on what you learned in the pre-physical-birth world. Think about the reasons that you feel you and this sibling were brought together. How does this information relate to your actual experience? Have you two learned the lessons from each other that you were meant to, or does more work need to be done?

6. Envision your sibling again, this time with a golden light around him. Thank him for choosing to be in your life, forgive him for pain caused, and bless him for all the lessons learned.

7. Take several deep breaths, and end the exercise. Write down your insights in the space provided.

MONTH 1

MONTH 2

MONTH 3

MONTH 4

MONTH 5

MONTH 6

MEDITATION 19

The Stepchild

TIME REQUIRED: *ten to fifteen minutes*

In today's world of blended families, a stepparent/stepchild relationship is a common occurrence. Unfortunately, equally common is the belief that this relationship must be problematic and ambivalent. Here's an exercise for stepparents that is intended to help create greater harmony in the family.

ॐ ॐ ॐ

1. Get comfortable, close your eyes and do the relaxation exercise.

2. Visualize your stepchild. Try to see past any disagreements, any behavioral issues to the child's basic self—a being wanting to be loved.

3. Acknowledge the importance of your stepchild in your life. Be aware that, just as with any other major relationship, you and your stepchild in all probability

had a before-birth agreement to come together in this lifetime. Ask yourself why. What has s/he got to teach you? What have you got to teach the child?

4.   See yourself saying to your stepchild, "I love you because . . ." Envision the child's happy reaction. See yourself giving him or her a loving gift. What is inside? Why have you chosen it?

5.   See your stepchild saying to you, "I love you because . . ." Let yourself enjoy what s/he is saying. Resolve to be even more lovable in the future. Watch as s/he gives you a gift. What is inside? Why do you think s/he has chosen to give it to you?

6.   Spend a few moments talking, resolving issues, vowing to make your family life together as beautiful as possible. Give each other a hug.

7.   End the exercise, and open your eyes. Write down your experiences in the space provided. Now go over and hug your stepchild in reality!

MONTH 1

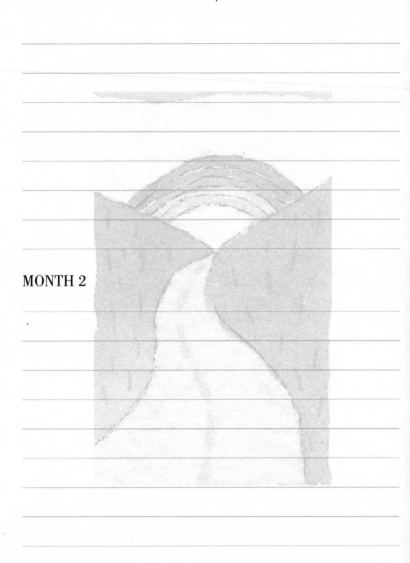

MONTH 2

MONTH 3

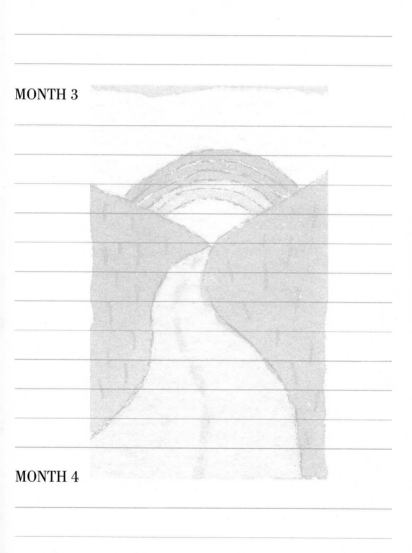

MONTH 4

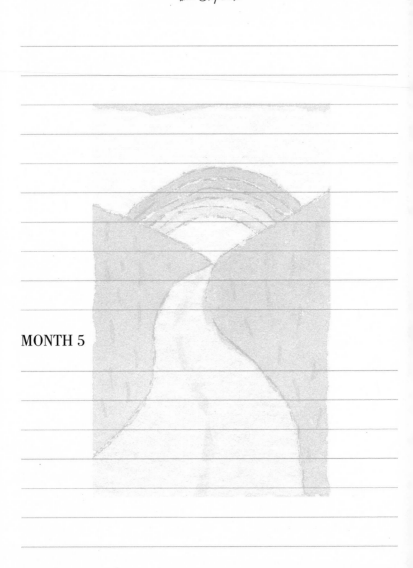

MONTH 5

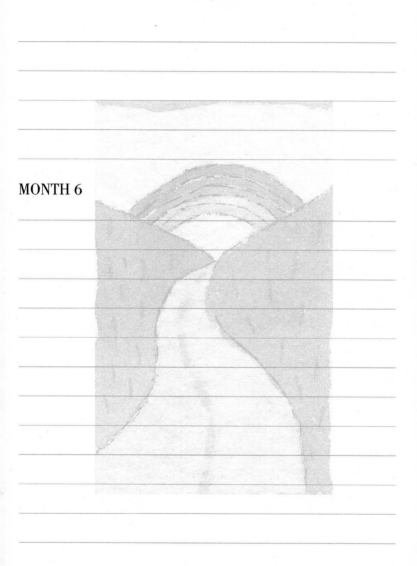

MONTH 6

MEDITATION 20

Fear Strikes Out

TIME REQUIRED: *five to ten minutes*

It is not unusual for parents to be gripped by a fear that something bad will happen to a happy, healthy child when they are away. But for both the parent's peace and happiness and for the continued well-being of the child, parents must work to discard these fearful beliefs. Children eventually pick up on those anxieties, and, ironically, can end up manifesting the very thing feared! Here's a meditation to help you break the cycle.

ॐ ॐ ॐ

1. Get comfortable, close your eyes, and do the relaxation exercise.

2. Affirm: "The source of my child's life is not me. It is God. My child's future is not dependent on me. It is dependent on God."

3. Envision your child totally surrounded by a safe, golden bubble. See him/her laughing, confident, secure, able to handle any situation.

4. Vow to do the best for your child as his/her physical parent. Beyond that, be willing to trust him/her to God's superior care.

5. End the exercise, open your eyes, and write your experiences in the space provided.

MONTH 1

MONTH 2

MONTH 3

MONTH 4

MONTH 5

MONTH 6

MEDITATION 21

The Parent Trap

TIME REQUIRED: *five to ten minutes*

Calling all children, young and old! It's such an easy, tempting trap for us to lament what our parents cannot or will not give us, while simultaneously being ungrateful or uncomfortable with accepting what they can and do give. Here's a way of springing that trap, and bringing a lot more gratitude to the relationship.

Note: even if your parents have gone to spirit, the meditation can still help heal the past.

శ్రీ శ్రీ శ్రీ

1. Get comfortable, close your eyes, and do the relaxation exercise.

2. Spend a few minutes meditating on all that your parents have given to you throughout your life. Think of concrete things like shelter, clothing, as well as emotional things like love and support.

3. Think of the single greatest gift your parents have given you—the gift of life. That alone deserves some thanks.

4. Silently bless your parents for what they have given you.

5. Think briefly of the things you feel they have withheld from you. In your mind, summon the images of your parents. Ask them why they have withheld these things. Were they unaware you needed them? Were they simply not able, given their personalities, to provide them? Did they feel it would be a mistake, for whatever reason, to give you what you wanted? Listen to what they have to say.

6. Do your best to release any longing for, or resentment surrounding, those things which your parents cannot or will not give to you.

7. Silently bless your parents for *not* giving you those things. Know that everything works for the best in this universe and that everything has its reasons.

8. End this meditation, open your eyes, and write your experience in the space provided.

MONTH 1

MONTH 2

MONTH 3

MONTH 4

MONTH 5

MONTH 6

MEDITATION 22

Strangers When We Meet

TIME REQUIRED: *five minutes*

American parents today are raising generations of youngsters with an unnatural and largely unwarranted fear of strangers. Obviously, certain commonsense advice like "never take candy from a stranger," or "never get into a stranger's car," apply, but in general, strangers mean no harm. The practice of totally ignoring them does nothing to ensure a child's safety, and it definitely contributes to him or her becoming a socially inept adult. Here's a meditation that will help break down some of those walls of fear, both for yourself and your children.

సామ సామ సామ

1. Get comfortable, close your eyes, and do the relaxation exercise.

2. Affirm: "All the people I see today are good, decent individuals wishing me no harm."

3. Plan on explaining to your children that, while certain safety guidelines must be followed, strangers can be seen simply as "friends they haven't met yet."

4. Resolve to greet the strangers in your day with a civilized, safe, "Hello," "Good morning," or other appropriate pleasantry.

5. Resolve to let your children see you doing this.

6. End this friendly exercise, and write your impressions in the space provided.

MONTH 1

MONTH 2

MONTH 3

MONTH 4

MONTH 5

MONTH 6

MEDITATION 23

Our Heavenly Father Knows Best

TIME REQUIRED: *five to ten minutes*

Parenthood need not be a mental tug-of-war between parents and their children. Forcing kids to accept certain behaviors and attitudes is as productive as trying to push square pegs into round holes. A better way is to stop pushing and instead yield to the heavenly Father who knows best. This is not a shirking of parental responsibility—it is simply an acknowledgment that God is the most effective teacher there is.

✄ ✄ ✄

1. Get comfortable, close your eyes, and do the relaxation exercise.

2. Visualize the situation with your child that is troubling you, and lay it before God. Now ask God to take over.

3. Put aside your own opinions. Be willing to let God's ideas prevail.

4. See those ideas as golden arrows flying through the air, winging their way not only to your children but also to yourself.

5. Express gratitude for Divine help, then end the exercise and write down your impressions in the space provided.

MONTH 1

MONTH 2

MONTH 3

_____

_____

_____

_____

_____

_____

_____

_____

_____

_____

_____

MONTH 4

_____

_____

_____

MONTH 5

MONTH 6

Meditations
on Work

ॐ ॐ ॐ

MEDITATION 24

Take This Job and Bless It!

TIME REQUIRED: *ten to fifteen minutes*

According to the media, apathy in the workplace is epidemic. Yet most people understand that a healthy relationship with their professional activities is an important aspect of successful living. Use this meditation to end professional apathy and to improve your relationship with the job or the career that you have right now.

ॐ ॐ ॐ

1. Get comfortable, close your eyes, and do the relaxation exercise.

2. In your meditative state, search your heart to reveal the reason(s) for your professional apathy. Do you feel that you deserve something better from life? Do you desire something more fulfilling and exciting than the work you have?

3. Now bless your work—the work you're doing right now. Bless it and be grateful for it. Realize that you

are doing God's perfect and important work, and visualize your workplace bathed in golden light.

4. Make a commitment to go beyond apathy and to self-create some new enthusiasm for your job or career as it is right now. Think of strategies to motivate yourself and enjoy yourself more. (If you are sitting at a desk all day, perhaps you should take more frequent breaks; instead of eating your lunch inside, go outside and eat at a nearby park. If your job is repetitive and undemanding, perhaps you can liven things up by setting more challenging goals of productivity for yourself. If your job involves dealing with the public, see how many new friends you can make within the course of each day.)

Note: Steps 3 and 4—blessing your work and vowing to give it all you've got—are powerful tools for change. One way or another, we always get out of our experience what we put into it, or, more eloquently stated, "Whatsoever a man soeth, that shall he also reap." (Gal. 6:7.) When you bless your work as it is right now and you go beyond apathy to generate new enthusiasm, your professional life will improve, even if the basic work stays the same. Simultaneously, you will also be sowing the seeds that will reap better professional opportunities in the future. The Universe appreciates, and rewards, perseverance and gratitude!

5. Take a few deep breaths, end the meditation, and open your eyes.

6. In the space provided, write down the reason(s) for your workplace apathy. Next, write an affirmation blessing your work. Finally, write down the strategies you've come up with to generate new enthusiasm for it.

MONTH 1

MONTH 2

MONTH 3

MONTH 4

MONTH 5

MONTH 6

MEDITATION

Changing Perspectives

TIME REQUIRED: *ten to fifteen minutes*

Perhaps due to the pressure of our times, perhaps due to the fact that we cannot always choose our coworkers, relationships on the job can be very stressful. Things can be especially difficult, even frightening, if we are working under a boss or manager who is intimidating or unappreciative. If you are in this position, this meditation can help you get a new perspective.

၇ၟ ၇ၟ ၇ၟ

1. Get comfortable, close your eyes, and do the relaxation exercise.

2. Summon up the image of the person you have a hard time dealing with. Now think of a specific time when he/she intimidated or upset you. (For ease in reading, we will address the person as "he.")

3. Remember the moment as accurately as you can. Play the scene in your mind as if you were watching a movie. Try to remember specific phrases used, (e.g.: "you're an idiot!") and specific gestures (e.g.: shaking a fist.)

4. Now run through the scene again—but this time see it in slow motion. See the person walking around with dinosaur-like steps, hear him say his phrase ("You're an idiot!" sounds really funny in slow motion), and watch him making his gesture (Shaking a fist isn't very threatening when it's done at snail speed.) See how ridiculous it all looks.

5. Now run through the scene again—but this time see it sped way up. See the person rushing around like a cartoon character, squeaking "You're an idiot!" and whizzing his impotent fist around in the air. Enjoy the silliness.

6. Now run through the scene again. This time, describe to yourself what happens in language that is completely factual and entirely devoid of emotion. "_____ came into my office. We talked a few minutes. He said 'You're an idiot' to me. He shook his fist. He left the room." Doesn't sound like the end of the world, does it?

7. Repeat: "_____ has no power over me. I am secure within myself and completely unafraid."

8. Envision the scene one last time. Send healing white light to both yourself and to the other person. Let it go forever.

9. Take a few deep breaths and end the exercise. Write down your impressions in the space provided.

MONTH 1

MONTH 2

MONTH 3

MONTH 4

MONTH 5

MONTH 6

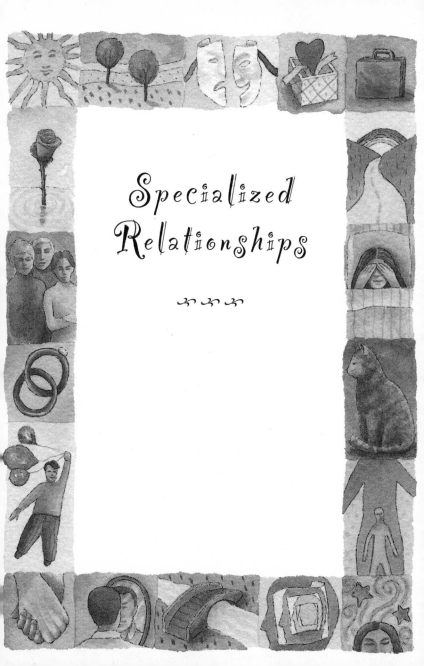

Specialized Relationships

✧ ✧ ✧

MEDITATION 26

And Toto, Too?
Yes, Toto, Too!

TIME REQUIRED: *ten to fifteen minutes*

The Golden Rule mandates us to love God and to care for one another. We believe that mandate should be extended to include a respectful and loving regard for all other species with whom we share the planet. As pet parents, the authors deeply appreciate and respect how other species contribute to our sense of health and well-being on a practical, day-to-day basis.

༄ ༄ ༄

1. Get comfortable, close your eyes, and do the relaxation exercise.

2. Try to remember various times when your life was enhanced by some nonhuman creature. Was a pet your bedside companion during a childhood illness? Were your spirits raised on a blue Monday by the cheerful song of a bird? Was visiting the ducks at a nearby pond a favorite recreational activity for

you and your parents? Did you believe you saw the face of God in the wings of a beautiful butterfly? Bless all the creatures on the planet.

3. Take a moment and select your personal favorite nonhuman species.

4. Take another moment to select your personal favorite creature from within that species—perhaps a current household pet or one from your childhood.

5. Visualize the creature standing before you bathed in golden light. Express gratitude to God for this loved one.

6. If possible, decide to do something special this very day for him or her. Special treats, new toys, stroking behind the ear are all appreciated! Even if your loved creature is deceased, you could decide to send a loving prayer his or her way.

7. End your meditation, open your eyes, and write your experience in the space provided.

Note: Each time you repeat this meditation, try selecting a different species—and a new favorite creature.

MONTH 1

MONTH 2

MONTH 3

MONTH 4

MONTH 5

MONTH 6

MEDITATION

Transcending Abuse

TIME REQUIRED: *ten to fifteen minutes*

The Scenario:

"I knew that Rick had grown up in a violent home. But he was sincere and disciplined, and I believed his violent roots need not soil our marriage. How wrong I was. The anger and rage Rick held for his father surfaced regularly and dramatically. Within six weeks of our marriage, I became an abused wife—physically, mentally, emotionally. I felt ashamed, guilty, desperate and didn't know what to do."

Abusive relationships are tragic, both for the victim and—less obviously—the perpetrator. Each case is unique, with its own root causes and best hope of cure. In many situations, psychological or marital counseling is a productive option. And in others, the only course of action is the abused partner leaving the relationship as swiftly as possible.

If you are in an abusive relationship, whatever you choose to do about it on the physical plane, the following exercise will help you release some pain and connect you with a Higher Power.

1. Make yourself comfortable, close your eyes, and do the relaxation exercise.

2. Visualize the person who is abusing you. See him/her covered with a dark shadow. Now see him/her step away from the shadow, and become separate from it.

3. Say silently, "_____ is separate from his/her deeds. I cannot love the deeds, but I can love and forgive _____."

4. Ask God to allow your loved one to forgive both him/herself and those towards whom he feels anger and rage.

5. Ask that your loved one be open to accepting God's forgiveness.

6. Visualize the dark shadow slowly disappearing and being bathed in a warm light of love.

7. End the meditation, open your eyes, and write your experience in the space provided.

MONTH 1

MONTH 2

MONTH 3

MONTH 4

MONTH 5

MONTH 6

MEDITATION 28

Out and Out

TIME REQUIRED: *ten minutes*

The Scenario:

"I met Nancy after dating a long list of women with whom I did not connect. Then she came along, and it seemed like a perfect fit. We had similar moral values, liked each other's friends and family, and shared the same taste in just about everything. I thought she was The One. But strangely, even after months of social dating, Nancy diligently avoided intimacy.

Finally, I found out why. Nancy revealed that we had even more in common than I had thought—we were both sexually attracted to women. When I asked why she was dating me, her answer was, 'I've never had a more perfect relationship, and I didn't want it to end. The only thing missing is the sexual attraction. I didn't want to lose you just because I'm a lesbian.'"

If this scenario (or a similar one involving a man) is occurring in your own life, here is an exercise that might help put things in perspective.

ॐ ॐ ॐ

1. Get comfortable, close your eyes, and do the relaxation exercise.

2. Visualize your gay/lesbian friend smiling lovingly at you. See him/her as being perfect the way he/she is. If you have any secret thoughts of changing his/her sexual orientation, lose it. For the most part, people are not gay/lesbian because they haven't found the right opposite sex partner. In most cases, sexual orientation is not a personal choice but a genetic determination.

3. Gratefully acknowledge and accept the love your gay/lesbian friend offers to you.

4. Silently vow to develop and encourage all of the good aspects of the relationship, while trying to release sexual desire for the person.

5. End the meditation, open your eyes, and write your experience in the space provided.

MONTH 1

MONTH 2

MONTH 3

MONTH 4

MONTH 5

MONTH 6

MEDITATION 29

The Bridge

TIME REQUIRED: *five to ten minutes*

In his powerful novel, *The Bridge of San Luis Rey*, Thornton Wilder speaks of a land of the living and a land of the dead—and the bridge between them being love.

This meditation will let you build your own bridge to someone you love who has gone to Spirit.

(*Note:* To make the exercise easier to read, we will call the loved one "she.")

సౌ సౌ సౌ

1. Get comfortable, close your eyes, and do the relaxation exercise.

2. Visualize yourself standing in front of a dark river, wanting to get across to the other bank but being unable to. Then create a bridge for yourself and

watch it materialize. It can be of any substance you want—stone, light, rainbow, vines, etc.

3. See yourself running joyfully over the bridge, happily expectant about what you will find on the other side.

4. You are now on the other side of the bridge. It is magical there, beautiful, peaceful. Someone is running towards you, calling your name. It is your beloved one. She looks radiant and wonderful.

5. Feel yourself embracing her. She feels solid, warm. Sense your love flowing into her and hers into you. Tell her how much you miss her. Tell her how much you love her. Let her know she is still important to you.

6. Now hear what she has to say. If you want to, ask questions about the nature of existence on the Other Side. Or perhaps you might want to ask if she has any advice for you to help you with your life on earth. Or maybe there's an undone task she would like you to do for her.

7. Promise you'll come back and visit soon. Give each other another hug.

8. Go back over the bridge.

9. Take a few deep breaths, open your eyes, and write about your experiences in the space provided.

MONTH 1

MONTH 2

MONTH 3

MONTH 4

MONTH 5

MONTH 6

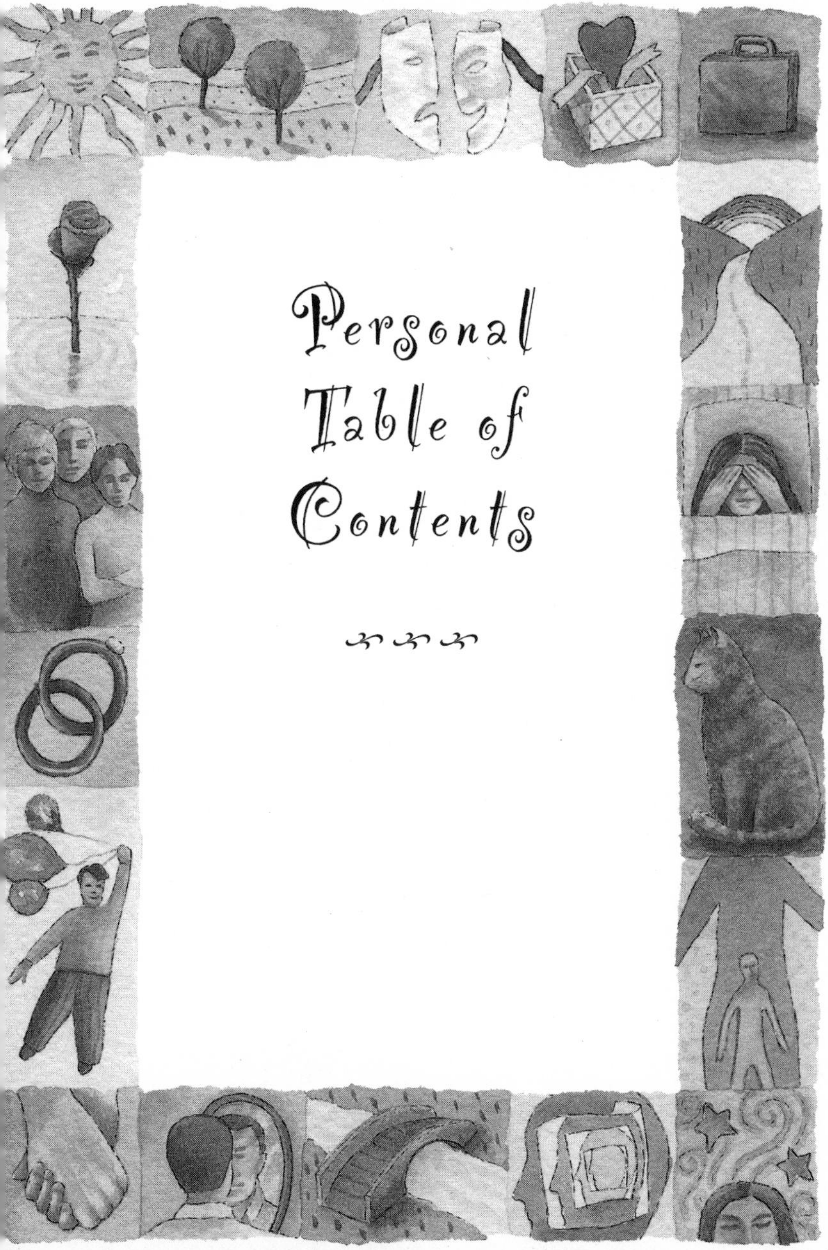

Personal Table of Contents

MONTH

1

MONTH 2

215

MONTH

MONTH 4

MONTH 5

MONTH 6

Suggested Reading

In any bookstore, you'll find an inspiring myriad of books on improving your relationship with yourself and with everyone else in your life. Here are a few we personally recommend:

Books on Improving Your Relationship with Yourself

The Meditation Journal and *Meditations for the 21st Century* by Mary Sheldon and Christopher Stone. These are our two earlier books, geared towards enhancing your spirit through a series of guided meditations.

Living in the Light by Shakti Gawain. A loving and inspiring blueprint for learning to trust your deepest self.

The Letters of the Scattered Brotherhood edited by Mary Strong. Published over half a century ago, this ever-fresh volume will help you connect to the unseen side of life.

The Care of the Soul and *The Re-Enchantment of Everyday Life* by Thomas Moore. These lovely and intelligent essays present provocative insights into the human condition.

Life 101 and *You Can't Afford the Luxury of a Negative Thought* by Peter McWilliams. These effervescent volumes are filled with humor, marvelous quotes, and sparkling ideas.

Chop Wood, Carry Water edited by Fields, Taylor, Weyler, and Ingrasci. This anthology on the Zen way of being is a fascinating and very readable tapestry of information.

You Can Heal Your Life by Louise Hay. This beautifully simple book resounds with positive energy.

BOOKS ON IMPROVING YOUR RELATIONSHIP WITH OTHERS

Loving Each Other by Leo Buscaglia. This man knew a lot about love and loving, and he shared it all in this warm volume.

How to Get More Love into Your Life by Alan Epstein, Ph.D. A strategy-a-day to promote beautiful relationships.

Getting the Love You Want by Harville Hendrix. A fascinating book about why we choose the people we do and how to make our choices work for us.

Whole Child/Whole Parent by Polly Berrien Berends. The world's most fantastic book about raising a child.

Soul Mates by Thomas Moore. The author of *The Care of the Soul* turns his attention outwards to loving relationships.

Men Are from Mars, Women Are from Venus by John Gray. Surely the most fascinating, fun, and thought-provoking volume on relationships ever. You'll never view your mate in the same way again!